All rights reserved. No part of this book may be used or reproduced in any manner whatsoever without written permission of the author, except in the case of brief quotations embodied in critical articles or review.

Back cover photo: Sally R. Chafee

Copyright © 2017 by Katharine Smith-Warren

ISBN 978-0-991256-0-1
Library of Congress Control Number: 20179 100 28
LCCN Imprint Name: Triple Creek Press Denver, Colorado

Is this how it will be?

Written and illustrated
by Katharine Smith-Warren

"...did they warn us about this freedom—
that there are no regulations—that we do
not run out of patience, we run out of time."

—JORIE GRAHAM, "WITH MOTHER IN THE KITCHEN"
THE NEW YORKER, DECEMBER 12, 2016

In memory of
William T. Chafee : 1931-1979
Peter Warren : 1938 -2015

It didn't seem real and still doesn't. Grieving the loss of a loved one is a painful experience. All losses hurt but the loss of a spouse or partner drastically alters our life.

I have had the sad experience of being widowed twice. My first husband died in an automobile accident after we were married eight years. I was thirty-four years old and we had a five year-old son. I remarried and after thirty-three years of marriage my second husband died after a long and debilitating illness.

Does that make me somehow more knowledgeable about loss and grief? Probably not. We all grieve in our own way. Now I am at the age when the losses are piling up in alarming numbers: parents, sibling, friends, relatives.

I kept a journal of the first year following my second husband's death and these paintings and words are from my journal. It is my hope that they may help others as they face this difficult time.

— Katharine

October

Good
Iceland, France, California, Alaska.

Not so good
doctors
therapists
nurses
emergency rooms
hospitals
palliative care
hospice

The Saturday night before you died
we looked at Caribbean cruises.

*I knew we wouldn't go,
maybe you did too.*

That weekend you were sleeping more and more. Our son came over to watch the Bronco game with you and you couldn't stay awake. Monday afternoon you fell asleep and didn't wake up.

Unresponsive.

The hospice nurse told us.

Four days and three nights
of watching your life slowly end.

Each day

I played your favorite music; Schubert and Bach. I filled your desk with pictures, your mother and sister, me in France, you and our son, the whole family last Easter. Our granddaughter sent a painting that I taped to your monitor.

Each night I reluctantly went to our bedroom to try to sleep, unsure if you would be alive in the morning. During the night I would get up several times, and go into your room to watch you. One night I crawled into the narrow hospital bed and lay next to you.

No response.

Did you know I was there?

The End

Thursday afternoon the time between
each breath lengthened and time slowed
as I heard our son walking up stairs after work.
We were together as your breath stopped.

.

You were gone.

Our son and I scattered your ashes
at our mountain cabin.

November

Every morning I woke up and looked next to me.

The Memorial

I sat in the balcony with the grandchildren at your memorial. I hardly remember it.

I lighted a memorial candle at church.

A step forward; I read a whole book
M Train by Patti Smith.

Christmas: Merry? No.

Bittersweet time with family.

Last Christmas you were in the hospital and
I wrote in my journal: "Worst Christmas ever."

I go ahead and plan to move.
Too many memories here.

I gave away the cash in your wallet to people on the streets. And your cigarettes.

You always worried about the homeless.

Reno our cat is a comfort.

January

New Years.
What will the year ahead be without you?

My grief is a constant, a hole in my life.
Going through your stuff. So many decisions.

I try not to fall into the hole. Instead let
the grief touch me. I feel it and then move ahead.

Moving, so much to do.
So much to dispose of.
What to take with me.
So many things, so many memories.

Your shell collection is packed and goes to the museum.

Saying goodbye to our home for twenty-three years.

New home. Feels right.

I have some friends over for dinner.

So very different without you.

March

Houston airport. On my way to Mexico.
Like a thousand pinpricks memories of our last trip
to Mexico. The restaurant where we splurged
on a fancy meal while waiting for our connecting flight.

Now I return with your ashes in my suitcase.

I return to the seaside village we visited for the past
eight years — everything the same but everything is
different, without you.

Late afternoon. I went to the beach and spread your ashes as the waves come in. Some blew back on me, some fell in the sand and some drifted into the ocean.

I went for a manicure with Angeles, who used to cut your hair. "Todos morimos," she says sadly.

On the way home I spent time alone in Mexico City. It was OK. Different but OK.

April

Kept busy fixing up my new home.

Everyone, friends and family, wants me to feel better. Why don't I? I go back to my grief counselor to talk.

Maybe the Victorians were right. Grieve for a year.
Black armbands and crepe over the front door.
Can it be six months? The waves of sadness come
but they don't knock me down.

When will spring come?

I am tired of winter.
You hated winter.

May

The loneliness of tea time.
And cocktail time.
And dinner alone.

I went to Costco for the first time without you.
When I saw the scooters parked in the entry

I was sad.

And I didn't park in the disabled space.

I sit alone at twilight and watch out my window at the dog walkers and runners on the way to the park. Spring slowly appears.

alone

June
July

Back at our cabin in the mountains.
Nature and beauty touch me.
Your walking stick stays by the door.

I went to a folk music potluck. Alone. It was OK.

I search for some wine at the cabin. All I find is the orange liquor you used to make margaritas. I am stunned to realize I will never have one of your special margaritas again.

Reread *The Year of Magical Thinking.* "Grief turns out to be a place none of us know until we reach it."

Still running into people who don't know.

Hard

August

Another trip, this time with the grandchildren and family. Back to Cape Cod where you and I went ten years ago.

Our son catches my favorite fish for dinner.
A family get-together with cousins without you.

Train to NY to visit friends. *alone*

September

I am a widow who lives alone.
My mother was alone for 30 years.

Our cat dies.

I join a book club.

I decide to spend six weeks in Mexico next winter.
I will rent my own place, near a friend.

I walk in the park in the beautiful autumn weather.
Young couples pass, holding hands.
Do they imagine that in 40 years they might wait
by the bedside as one of them dies?

I return to Garden of the Gods in Colorado Springs. You fell once, we had to have room service for meals but it was a beautiful September weekend. We drove home the long way through the mountains.
It was our last trip.

I thought it would make me sad to return but I had a realization: I did a good thing in taking you there.
I can feel good about that.

I couldn't save you.

but I could make you happy.

I go on a weekend retreat and admire someone with blue nail polish. She offers to paint my nails blue.

October

A friend's husband dies suddenly.
Another friend's husband dies after a long illness.

I wake up one morning and I feel different.
As if a fog has lifted.

I start painting again.

I got through your birthday, September 30.
Now I wait for the anniversary of your death
this month.

Dinner with family and grandchildren
on the anniversary. Indian food.
One of your favorites.

I spend time with a friend who is a caregiver for her husband. She is feeling the weight of it, just as I did.

I don't tell her she will go from a full time, exhausting and challenging time to nothing.
There is busyness but not the wholeness of taking care of someone you love.

It has been a year.

I am a different person.
I dreamed of you last night. We were vacationing in a suburban-style large house.
We agreed it wasn't our kind of place.

You were always in another room.

Katharine Smith-Warren
is an artist and writer
living in Denver, Colorado.

www.ingramcontent.com/pod-product-compliance
Lightning Source LLC
Chambersburg PA
CBHW042100290426
44113CB00005B/109